Army

GREEN BERETS

by Jack David

BELLWETHER MEDIA ★ MINNEAPOLIS, MN

Library of Congress
David, Jack, 1968–
  Army Green Berets / by Jack David.
      p. cm. — (Torque. Armed forces)
  Includes bibliographical references and index.
  Summary: "Full color photography accompanies exciting
information about the Army Green Berets. The combination
of high-interest subject matter and light text is intended for
students in grades 3 through 7"—Provided by publisher.
  ISBN-13: 978-1-60014-263-5 (hbk. : alk. paper)
  ISBN-10: 1-60014-263-X (hbk. : alk. paper)
  1. United States. Army. Special Forces—Juvenile literature. I.
Title.
  UA34.S64D38 2009
  356'.167—dc22   2008035644

021510   1159

CONTENTS

★ ★ ★

★ ★ ★

SAFE

Chapter One

WHAT ARE THE GREEN BERETS?

The Green Berets are some of the United States Army's most highly trained soldiers. The official name of the Green Berets is the U.S. Army Special Forces. They perform some of the most difficult **missions** for the army.

The Green Berets specialize in several kinds of missions. They work with and train the fighting forces of other countries. They gather information on terrorists and prevent attacks. This is called **counterterrorism**. They also carry out small, quick attacks on important enemy locations. They can get in, attack, and get out before an enemy even knows they were there.

Every Green Beret must speak at least one foreign language fluently. Common languages among Green Berets include Arabic, Chinese, Russian, and Spanish.

Chapter Two

WEAPONS AND GEAR

M4 carbine

A Green Beret needs a weapon that is easy to use on the move. The M-4 **carbine** is a Green Beret's main gun. It is light, powerful, and accurate.

Green Berets must stay on course and in contact during missions. They use **global positioning systems (GPS)** to find their way to specific locations. Special long-range radios help them talk to other soldiers and send text messages.

A variety of other equipment is helpful to Green Berets. **Re-breathers** allow Green Berets to breathe underwater. **Night-vision goggles** help them see even on the darkest of nights. They may carry climbing gear, rafts, **kayaks**, and other equipment to help them travel through an area.

Green Berets travel on military aircraft. Helicopters such as the AH-60 Blackhawk and the MH-67 Chinook carry them wherever they need to go. They know how to jump out of planes at very high **altitudes** and parachute to the ground. They wear special High-Altitude Low-Opening (HALO) helmets to help them breathe in the thin air.

When parachuting, Green Berets wait as long as possible to open their chutes. This is dangerous, but it prevents enemies from detecting them.

Chapter Three

LIFE AS A GREEN BERET

All Green Berets begin their training at Fort Bragg, North Carolina.

It takes a lot of courage, skill, and hard work to become a Green Beret. They're the brightest and the most skilled soldiers the Army has to offer. For Green Berets, **basic training** is just the beginning of their education.

Future Green Berets start the Special Operations Preparation and Conditioning Course after basic training. There they go through tough strength and fitness training. They also learn to **navigate** through any kind of terrain. Next, they go to Special Forces Assessment and Selection. They are tested on their judgment and leadership under stressful situations.

Those who make it this far enter the final phase of training, the Special Forces Qualification Course. This five-part course focuses more on survival skills, **unconventional warfare**, language training, and other special skills. After this, a soldier becomes a Green Beret.

Green Berets have to make many decisions on their own. They may go days or weeks without contact with their superior officers. They have to rely on their own judgment.

Green Berets often work undercover. They pretend to be ordinary citizens of other countries.

Green Berets work in teams stationed around the world. Each team of 12 Green Berets includes a commander, weapons specialists, and medical specialists. They may stay behind enemy lines for months at a time. No matter where they're stationed, Green Berets are always ready to perform their missions to keep the United States safe.

altitude—distance above sea level

basic training—the combination of drills, tests, and military training that new enlisted members of the United States Army must go through

carbine—a short-barreled repeating rifle

counterterrorism—a military mission designed to discover or prevent terrorist activity

global positioning system (GPS)—a device that uses satellites orbiting Earth to determine a precise position on the globe

kayak—a small, motorless boat similar to a canoe

mission—a military task

navigate—to find one's way in unfamiliar terrain

night-vision goggles—a special set of glasses that allow the wearer to see at night

re-breather—a device that allows Green Berets to breathe while underwater, helping them to move undetected through lakes and rivers

unconventional warfare—non-traditional fighting; unconventional warfare often includes short, hit-and-run attacks on important enemy locations and bases.

TO LEARN MORE

★ ★ ★

AT THE LIBRARY

David, Jack. *United States Army*. Minneapolis, Minn.: Bellwether, 2008.

Glaser, Jason. *Green Berets*. Mankato, Minn.: Capstone, 2007.

Nobleman, Marc Tyler. *Green Berets in Action*. New York: Bearport, 2008.

ON THE WEB

Learning more about the Green Berets is as easy as 1, 2, 3.

1. Go to www.factsurfer.com.

2. Enter "Green Berets" into the search box.

3. Click the "Surf" button and you will see a list of related Web sites.

With factsurfer.com, finding more information is just a click away.

INDEX

★ ★ ★